You Can Do It!
The Overcomer's Journal
Dr. Brunetta Nelson

Imprint Productions Inc.

You Can Do It
The Overcomer's Journal

Dr. Brunetta Nelson

ISBN-13: 978-1-956884-07-4

Dedication

I dedicate this book to the most loving parents - the late Alphonzo Nelson, Sr., and Pastor Doris Virginia Hall-Nelson, and my baby sister whom heaven has already claimed, Sylvia, my elder siblings, Tyrone & wife Kim, Debra, Alphonzo Jr., Barbara & husband-the late Stanley Hester, Angela, Antonio, the nieces, nephews, cousins, uncles, aunts, friends, and team Imprint Productions, Inc. and our Associates.

table of contents

You sat in the driver's seat and decided what journey you'd take. You did it then and "You Can Do It!" again.

Come with me. I want to quench your thirst, pour some juice into your journey!

Let me coax you, tease you, lift you, please you, push you, pull you and shake you from the bottom up! You ushered in this day with pure effervescence, bubbling over with curiosity, expectations, and anticipation! Your imagination is lit!

Indulge with me for a moment. Let me take you back to that first slap when you were born. When the doctor hit you on your bottom immediately after your arrival from the birth canal, that was your first touch to stimulate a response. This book is synonymous with that aggressive stimulation, that 'laying on of hands.' The vitals, signs of life, sounds, and movement that sets you apart for God's holy use. That first cry, that sound of I'm here, and I'm alive! The universe is waiting to move at your request. Say something, do something, create something.

I want to slap you into your next life figuratively! I want you to die to the failures, the letdowns, the setbacks, the neglect, the omissions. I want to be a witness as you're lifted from the tomb and resurrected. Welcome to the universe!

Before we step into our power space, unplug with me, and download a new meta program. Gift me with your most intimate and private thoughts. Let me speak to the core of your comprehension. I want this moment to be the beginning of the new you, the you that believes in yourself and your power to live again, dream again, stand again, succeed again, no matter what the again may be.

Fall seven times and get up eight. After a failure or setback, there are usually questions. How do I move from wanting to get back up to actually getting back up? How do I start over? Can I build again, can I write again, can I love again? Thanks, I am so glad you asked.

Take a few cleansing breaths, sip some water to refresh your brain, and get comfortable. We are going to excavate your inner artifacts and unearth the treasures already inside of you! Your inheritance, the jewels you wear in your crown. You were born for this moment, it's yours for the taking. I labored in love to get this message to you!! Failure is not an option; no grit, no pearl.

Rock with me! You know how we roll. From time to time, we all must endure a breakdown with all its organized chaos. It gives us the clarity and a road map to get to the breakthrough. The juice in your journey gets stirred up, like a pot of grits, boosting the elixir until juice boost stirring, a spike, and some juice boost! Please get this, your arrival is spectacular, but that's not what's compelling; it's the juicy journey. People want to know about the failures, the challenges that couldn't defeat you; how you lost everything but failure was not an option, how you cried all night but put on the can-do face in the morning, how you were left with three kids but you were determined to make a meaningful life for them, how you flunked out of school but you didn't quit, how you slept in the car but still kept looking for the dream, how the house was repossessed, but you pressed on, how you didn't know where the next meal would come, how you didn't want to exist anymore but you knew living life would be greater!

When Tyler Perry shares his journey, people gravitate to the journey. He shares how he was homeless and sleeping in cars. We celebrate him, but it's the juicy Journey that moves us to hope, to plan, to execute, and to rethink our possibilities to excel, to be spectacular!! Honey, the juice is in the journey. Later in the book, I'll share years of my journey in detail and how I reinvented Brunetta! I'll also provide some space for you to share your journey. Even now, as I am writing, I'm thinking of you and how we will celebrate each other! I want you all in with me, just us! It's getting hot in here. Overcomers know that there must be a revelation, an application, and then the transformation.

Let's move on! You are an overcomer because you are still here, reading me, and you were on my mind. Somehow I knew you would be turning these pages, and engaging this conversation with me. By now, I know that the adrenaline is high, your mind wants more, and you're ready to rewrite the narrative.

Overcomers don't settle, they get up, they decide….. Don't ever count an overcomer out; we bounce up, we have more lives than a cat, and we will always get back on the saddle! Overcomers know that if you fall 7 times, you get back up 8 times. We might feel stuck, and sometimes fall harder than we could imagine, but it's in our core to get up! Awwww, I sense another mind shift!

Yes, shift with me; you were born for this moment to shift the gear, change the course, make the mark, leave a trail……. Your climate, your region, and your zone have changed; you've prevailed. The conditions are just right, you're onto another aspect of life. You Can Do It! Overcomers write their own story, blaze the trails, strike the match, hit the ball out of the park. We break the glass ceilings, baby!

Day 1

You're not alone; overcomers know that God is with them and for them.

Nelson Mandela was no stranger to struggle. He was once quoted as saying, "I learned that courage was not the absence of fear, but the triumph over it." After spending 27 years in prison for fighting against an injustice called apartheid, Nelson Mandela was freed and eventually elected as the first black president of South Africa. Despite all the challenges he faced, he never gave up hope because he knew God was with him and for him. He knew he could do it with God's help.

How has your faith helped you overcome challenges in your life?

Day 2

You are not your circumstances; overcomers know that they can change their circumstances.

Oprah Winfrey is one of the most famous women in the world. She came from humble beginnings, born to a teenage mother who was unmarried and living in poverty. She had been told her entire life that she was not smart enough, not pretty enough, and would never amount to anything. But Oprah didn't believe what others said about her. She knew she could change her circumstances and went on to become one of the most successful talk show hosts of all time. Oprah was able to change her circumstances through hard work and determination. She has also accomplished many other phenomenal things in her life, including becoming a billionaire businesswoman. Oprah's life has proven that circumstances are just that, circumstances, but they do not define you or determine your destiny.

What can you do to change your current circumstances?

Day 3

You have what it takes; overcomers know that they have the power within them to succeed.

John D. Rockefeller was born in 1839 to a poor family in upstate New York. He was one of six children and his father died when he was just a teenager. John started working as a clerk in a mercantile business at the age of 16, and then went on to start his own business. By the time he was in his early 20s, he had become one of the richest men in America. Rockefeller became famous for his business acumen and his success in the oil industry. He was also known for his philanthropy, giving away millions of dollars to charity. Even though he faced many challenges and obstacles in his life, John D. Rockefeller rose to fame and succeeded in life.

What do you think it was that helped John D. Rockefeller succeed when so many others with his background were failing?

Day 4

You are not your mistakes; overcomers know that they can learn from their mistakes.

Maria Martinez was born into a family of poverty in 1887. Her father died when she was young, and her mother was unable to care for all her children, so Maria went to live with her grandparents. As a young woman, she married a man who was abusive and alcoholic. Her life decision in choosing a mate could have completely derailed her destiny. But despite all the challenges she faced in her life, Maria rose above them.

When she was 26, Maria traveled to Santa Fe, New Mexico, to participate in an art show. There, she met an art dealer who encouraged her to keep making pottery. Maria returned home and started making even more elaborate pieces of pottery, which she began selling through mail-order catalogs. Her pottery became so popular that the president of the United States, Franklin D. Roosevelt, invited her to exhibit her work at the White House in 1941. Eventually, Maria became famous for helping to revive the traditional art of Pueblo pottery across the United States.

What perceived mistakes have you made in your life? What have you learned from them?

Day 5

Your story may not be what you want for your life; overcomers know they have the power to rewrite their story.

Kim Phuc was born on June 8, 1963, in the village of Trang Bang, South Vietnam. When she was only nine years old, her village was bombed by the North Vietnamese Army. In the panic and chaos that ensued, Kim was running away from the bombs with her cousins when she was injured by a napalm bomb. The napalm melted through her clothes and burned her skin, causing horrific injuries. Kim was photographed fleeing the scene, naked and screaming in agony.

The photograph of Kim Phuc became one of the most iconic images of the Vietnam War. For many years, Kim lived with her scars, both physically and emotionally. She had to have dozens of surgeries to try to repair the damage done to her skin. It wasn't until she met a Canadian journalist named Nick Ut that she began to heal emotionally. Ut encouraged her to tell her story and use her experience as a symbol of hope for peace.

Kim Phuc has since become a world-renowned peace activist. She has traveled all over the world to speak about the importance of peace and forgiveness. She is also an advocate for children's rights and has started several charities to help children affected by war and violence. She knows that you have the power to write the ending you desire.

What part of your story needs to be rewritten? How will you rewrite it?

Day 6

Your life struggles are not for nothing; overcomers know the journey is worth it.

When she was just a young girl, Marina Silva's mother died from illness. Her father was forced to raise Marina and her siblings on his own, and they faced many hardships as a result. Marina never had an easy life, but she was always determined to fight for what she believed in.

In the early 1980s, Marina became involved in politics and started working for several of environmental organizations. She quickly rose through the ranks, and by the 1990s she had become one of Brazil's most influential politicians. In 2003, she was appointed Minister of the Environment, and she served in that role for five years.

Marina Silva is known for her dedication to environmental causes. She has spoken out against deforestation, climate change, and the exploitation of natural resources. She has also been a vocal advocate for social justice and human rights. After leaving politics in 2010, Marina founded her own political party, the Rede Sustentabilidade (Sustainable Network).

What struggles have you experienced that you now know are making your life more worth living?

Day 7

You have heard people say that the struggle is real; overcomers know that struggle can be turned into strategy that leads to success.

Jesse Itzler is the co-founder of Marquis Jet, one of the world's largest private jet companies. He is also the founder of Zico Coconut Water, which he sold for a reported $200 million. Jesse is a self-proclaimed "serial entrepreneur" and has been involved in several; of different businesses over the years.

Jesse's success didn't come easy; he worked hard for everything he has achieved. When he was just starting out in business, Jesse was living in his van and sleeping on friends' couches. He would do anything to get ahead, and he was always willing to take risks.

Jesse's story is one of determination and perseverance. He never gave up, even when things were tough. He knows that the only way to achieve success is to grind it out and never give up.

What are you doing today to turn your past struggles into strategies that will get you closer to tomorrow's goals?

Day 8

You may be faced with so many difficulties that it's easy to feel like you are not strong enough; overcomers know that feelings can and do lie, so they rise above their feelings to greater things in life.

Nigerian - American Imelme Umana became the first black woman elected to be a member of the Harvard Law Review in 2017. Umana immigrated to America from Nigeria with her family when she was just five years old. Her father passed away shortly after they arrived in the United States, and her mother had to work two jobs to support the family.

Umana faced many challenges growing up, but she never let them stop her from achieving her goals. She worked hard in school and was determined to go to college. She ended up attending Harvard University, where she graduated with honors.

Umana is now a lawyer and an advocate for social justice. She is using her story to inspire other young people to pursue their dreams, regardless of the obstacles she overcame..

What difficult things have you faced in your life? How have you used those experiences to become a better person?

Day 9

Your childhood may have been surrounded by pain;
overcomers know that pain can serve a powerful purpose in
helping to build our endurance.

Kristin Anderson was born with a congenital heart defect and has spent her entire life dealing with health problems. As a child, she underwent multiple open-heart surgeries and was often in and out of the hospital. Kristin's health problems made it difficult for her to lead a normal childhood.

Despite all the challenges she faced, Kristin never gave up. She was determined to live a full and happy life. In 2009, she founded the nonprofit organization A Younique Foundation, which provides financial assistance to young adults with congenital heart defects.

Kristin's story is one of hope and resilience. She has overcome so much in her life, and she is using her experiences to help others..

What painful experiences have you faced in your life? How
have you overcome them? What has been the most difficult
thing you have ever faced?

Day 10

You may have people in your life that seem to impede your progress; overcomers know that it's important to stay focused on their goals and not let others discourage them.

Walt Disney was one of the most successful American entrepreneurs of the 20th century. He was the creator of many cartoons and the co-founder of The Walt Disney Company. He played a major role in the development of animation and theme parks worldwide.

Disney's childhood was marked by poverty and hardship. His father was an abusive alcoholic, and his family was often on the brink of financial ruin. Despite all of this, Disney was able to find success. He started his own animation studio, and he went on to create some of the most popular films and characters in history.

Disney's story is a reminder that anyone can overcome their circumstances and find success. No matter how difficult your childhood was, you can use your experiences to fuel your drive to achieve your dreams.

What can you learn from the tough times in your life? How will those lessons help you in your journey to success?

Day 11

You may feel oppressed because of injustice or unfair treatment in your life; overcomers know that barriers and obstacles can be broken down if you are willing to fight for what is right.

Diane Nash is a civil rights leader who was born in Chicago in 1938. She was one of the founders of the Student Nonviolent Coordinating Committee (SNCC), which played a pivotal role in the civil rights movement. Diane was also one of the original Freedom Riders, a group of activists who rode buses into the American South to protest segregation.

Diane Nash's work in the civil rights movement helped to bring about major changes in American society. She is a reminder that even when the odds seem insurmountable, you can make a difference if you are willing to stand up for what is right.

What injustices have you faced in your life? How have you fought against them? What difference do you hope to make in the world?

Day 12

You might feel like giving up when things get tough; overcomers know that it's important to persevere and never give up on yourself.

Kimora Lee Simmons is a supermodel, fashion designer, and television personality. She is the founder of the fashion brand Baby Phat, which she sold for over $140 million. Kimora was born in St. Louis, Missouri, to an African-American father and a Korean mother.

Kimora's childhood was far from easy. Her father was absent from her life, and her mother was struggling to make ends meet. When Kimora was 10 years old, she was sent to live with her father in Japan. This experience was very difficult for her, and she considered giving up on her dreams of becoming a model.

Fortunately, Kimora did not give up on herself. She went on to have a hugely successful career in the fashion industry. She is now a mother of three and a successful businesswoman.

What are your dreams and goals for the future? How can you use Kimora's story to gain momentum and encouragement?

Day 13

You may be exhausted from all the weight you are carrying; overcomers know that it's important to release the baggage of the past and live in the present.

Brené Brown is a research professor at the University of Houston. She has spent the past two decades studying courage, vulnerability, shame, and empathy. Her work has helped to change the way we think about these topics.

Brené has experienced a lot of pain and hardship in her life. She was sexually assaulted as a young woman, and she has also dealt with anxiety and depression. Despite all of this, Brené has been able to find healing and joy.

In her book, Rising Strong, Brené talks about the importance of releasing the baggage of the past and living in the present. She says, "You have to walk through your story before you can write the next chapter."

What are some of the things you need to let go of to move forward? How can Brené's story help you on your own journey of healing?

Day 14

You might feel like you're not good enough; overcomers know that it's important to love and accept yourself just the way you are.

Iyanla Vanzant is an author, motivational speaker, and television personality. She is the host of the OWN show Iyanla: Fix My Life, where she helps people to improve their lives. Iyanla was born in Brooklyn, New York, and she had a difficult childhood. She was sexually abused by her father and she became pregnant at the age of 16.

Despite all the challenges she has faced, Iyanla has been able to create a life that she loves. In her book, Peace from Broken Pieces, she talks about the importance of self-love and acceptance. She says, "You have to love yourself before you can fully love anyone else."

What are some of the things you need to do in order to love and accept yourself? How can Iyanla's story help you on your own journey to self-love?

Day 15

You might feel like you're all alone; overcomers know that it's important to find your tribe and surround yourself with supportive people.

The story of WhatsApp cofounders Jan Koum and Brian Acton is one of rags to riches. The two men met while working at Yahoo, and they bonded over their shared love of programming. In 2009, they decided to start their own business together.

They were rejected by numerous investors before finally finding a home at Sequoia Capital. In 2014, Facebook acquired WhatsApp for $19 billion. This was a life-changing event for both Jan and Brian, and they both became millionaires overnight.

Despite their newfound wealth, the two men have remained grounded and humble. They continue to work together on WhatsApp, and they are both dedicated to making the app a success.

What are some of the things you need to feel supported and successful? Who is your tribe? What can you do together that is mutually beneficial to achieve your combined goals?

Day 16

You might be feeling trapped in your own body; overcomers know that it's important to love and appreciate your body just the way it is.

The story of Ashley Graham is one of self-love and acceptance. Ashley is a model, and she has been in the industry for over 10 years. She has appeared on the cover of magazines like Vogue, Elle, and Harper's Bazaar.

Ashley is considered to be plus-size, and she has been a vocal advocate for body positivity. In 2016, she became the first plus-size model to appear on the cover of the Sports Illustrated swimsuit issue.

In her book, A New Model: What Confidence, Beauty, and Power Really Look Like, Ashley talks about the importance of loving and accepting your body just the way it is. She says, "Your body is not an apology."

What are some of the things you need to do in order to love and accept your body? How can Ashley's story help you on your own journey to self-acceptance?

Day 17

You might feel like you're stuck in a rut; overcomers know that it's important to take risks and step out of your comfort zone.

In his book, The Lean Startup, Eric Ries talks about the importance of taking risks and stepping out of your comfort zone. He says, "The only way to win is to learn faster than anyone else."

Eric's story is one of taking risks and learning from failures. He is the co-founder of IMVU, and he has also worked with startups like LinkedIn and Twitter. In 2009, he published The Lean Startup, which quickly became a bestseller.

In The Lean Startup, Eric talks about the importance of taking risks and learning from your failures. He says, "The only way to win is to learn faster than anyone else."

What are some of the things you need to do in order to take risks and learn from your failures? How can Eric's story help you on your own journey to success?

Day 18

You might feel like everyone else has passed you up; overcomers know that it's important to believe in yourself and your abilities.

John Paul DeJoria is the perfect example of a man who didn't give up on his dreams. John Paul DeJoria is the co-founder of John Paul Mitchell Systems and Patrón Spirits Company. He didn't come to success and fortune until after he turned 50 years old, but that didn't stop him from achieving his goals.

John Paul's story is one of determination and perseverance. He was born into a family of migrant workers, and he himself worked as a janitor and car wash attendant before starting his own business. He was known for saying, "The only way to fail is to give up."

What are some of the things you need to do in order to achieve your dreams? How can John Paul DeJoria's story help you on your own journey to success?

Day 19

You might feel like life keeps knocking you down; overcomers know that it's important to get back up and keep going.

George McLaurin was born in Oklahoma in 1911. He was the son of former slaves, and he grew up during a time of great racial segregation. For 33 years, he had taught at Oklahoma's historically all-black institution, Langston University. He held a master's degree in education from the University of Kansas and had previously worked as a professor there. However, when McLaurin applied to the doctoral program at Oklahoma University, he was denied because of his race.

Though he was more than 60 years of age when he first applied in 1948, he decided to take the issue to court. And though he won when a federal court ruled that not letting him enroll was unconstitutional, it would be a few more years before he realized his dream.

He was admitted to OU but was tasked with learning in a closet that overlooked the room where his classmates sat. He had different mealtimes and tables in the lunchroom and a different table in the library. Despite the difficulties, George McLaurin persevered, and the Supreme Court ruled that he must receive the same treatment — not just "equal" treatment — as his peers at OU.

What are some of the things you need to do in order to achieve your dreams? How can George McLaurin's story help you on your own journey to success?

Day 20

You might feel like giving up is your only option; overcomers know that it's important to keep going and never give up.

Taraji P. Henson is one of the most successful actresses in Hollywood today. She has starred in films like The Curious Case of Benjamin Button, Hidden Figures, and Empire. In addition to her acting career, she has also directed several films.

Despite her success, Taraji has struggled with depression for many years. In a 2016 interview with People Magazine, she said, "I was suicidal. I was on drugs. I was searching for something that could make me happy."

Thankfully, Taraji was able to get help and overcome her depression. She now uses her experiences to help others who are struggling with mental health issues.

What can you learn from Taraji's story? How can it help you on your own journey to success?

Day 21

You might feel like you have way less than what it takes to make it in life; overcomers know that it's important to believe in yourself and your abilities.

Eric Thomas is a world-renowned motivational speaker. He is the author of several books, including The Secret to Success and The Power of Broke. He has also been featured on TED Talks, Oprah, and The Steve Harvey Show.

Despite his success, Eric Thomas struggled for many years. He was raised by a single mother who was addicted to drugs. He dropped out of high school and spent time being homeless. It wasn't until he met a man who told him he had the potential to be great that Eric decided to turn his life around.

He went back to school, got his GED, and then went on to get a bachelor's degree, a master's degree, and a doctorate. He is now one of the most successful motivational speakers in the world.

What can you learn from Eric Thomas' story? How can it help you on your own journey to success?

Day 22

You might feel like you're alone; overcomers know that it's important to connect with others who have similar goals and dreams.

Drew Brees is one of the most successful quarterbacks in NFL history. He has led the New Orleans Saints to a Super Bowl victory, and he has been named the NFL MVP twice.

Despite his success, Drew Brees struggled in his early years. He was passed over by every team in the NFL Draft, and many people told him he wasn't good enough to play professional football.

Thankfully, Brees didn't listen to the doubters. He stayed the course and signed with the San Diego Chargers and went on to have an incredible career. In 2012, he set the record for the most passing yards in a single season.

What things in your life do you need to stay the course for? How will this help you on your journey to success?

Day 23

You might feel like you will never get past your past; overcomers know that it's important to learn from your mistakes and move on.

Chuck Colson was a political strategist and a member of President Richard Nixon's inner circle. He was known as one of the most ruthless men in Washington.

Despite his success, Chuck Colson struggled with a number of personal demons. He was an alcoholic and had a gambling problem. He was also involved in the Watergate scandal, which led to him serving time in prison.

Thankfully, Colson was able to turn his life around after he went to prison. He became a born-again Christian and started a ministry for prisoners. He is now considered one of the most influential evangelical Christians in America.

What personal demons do you need to overcome? What steps will you take to use them to help others?

Day 24

You might feel like everything is stacked against you and you will never achieve your dreams; overcomers know that it's never too late to pursue your goals.

Ruth Bader Ginsburg is one of the most influential Supreme Court Justices in American history. She has been a powerful voice for gender equality and women's rights.

Despite her success, Ruth Bader Ginsburg struggled early in her career. She was denied a clerkship by Justice Felix Frankfurter because she was a woman. She was also told by a dean at Columbia Law School that it was a waste of time for her to be there because she would never find a job as a lawyer.

Thankfully, Ginsburg didn't let these setbacks stop her. She went on to become the first tenured female professor at Columbia Law School and eventually a Supreme Court Justice.

What obstacles have you faced in your life? How did you overcome them? What can you learn from Ruth Bader Ginsburg's story?

Day 25

You might feel like your mistakes are too public for you to ever overcome them; overcomers know that it's important to learn from your mistakes and move on.

Tiger Woods is one of the most successful golfers in history. He has won 14 major championships, and he is widely considered to be one of the greatest golfers of all time.

Despite his success, Tiger Woods has faced many challenges in his life. In 2009, he was involved in a highly publicized cheating scandal that led to the end of his marriage. He was also arrested for DUI in 2017.

Woods has admitted that he made some mistakes, but he has also said that he has learned from them. He is now focused on being better in all areas of his life.

What can you learn from Tiger Woods' story? What decisions will you make that will help you move on?

Day 26

You might feel like you can't pursue your dreams because you have too many responsibilities; overcomers know that it's important to set priorities and focus on what's most important.

Elon Musk is the founder of Tesla, SpaceX, and several other companies. He is widely considered to be one of the most innovative and successful entrepreneurs in history.

Despite his success, Elon Musk has faced many challenges in his life. He has had to deal with production issues at Tesla, criticism from the media, and short sellers who are betting against Tesla's stock. Many times, he had to work 80 hours per week to maintain his success.

Musk has said that he sometimes feels like he is "stuck in a video game where the goal is to not die." But he also knows that he needs to keep going because he has a responsibility to his employees and shareholders. Because of his determination, he is now one of the richest men in the world.

What are your priorities? What are you willing to do to achieve your goals?

Day 27

You might feel like there is just one thing after another in the way of your dream; overcomers know that it's important to persevere to achieve their dreams.

When Jim Carrey was fifteen, he dropped out of school to support his family. His father had lost his job, and the family was struggling to make ends meet. Carrey took a job as a janitor at a factory, but he was determined to pursue his dream of becoming a comedian.

Carrey didn't have much money, so he could only afford to take the bus to comedy clubs. He would often sneak into clubs to watch comics perform, and he even performed himself on occasion.

Eventually, Carrey's hard work paid off. He was discovered by a talent agent, and he went on to have a very successful career in Hollywood.

What are you willing to do to achieve your dreams? What sacrifices are you willing to make? What risks are you willing to take?

Day 28

You might feel stuck when things get tough; overcomers know that it's important to persist even when things are difficult.

Serena Williams is one of the most successful tennis players in history. She has won 23 Grand Slam singles titles, and she is widely considered to be one of the greatest athletes of all time.

Despite her success, Williams has faced many challenges in her life. She has dealt with injuries, racism, and sexism throughout her career. In 2017, she was involved in a controversial U.S. Open final where she was accused of cheating.

Williams has said that she sometimes feels like giving up, but she knows that she can't. She is determined to fight for what she believes in and to be a role model for other women. She has recently made the decision to bring her career to a close. In her first-person essay written for vogue she writes that she is not retiring, instead she is evolving.

What are you fighting for? What are you willing to persist through? Why is it important for you to overcome your challenges? How will you evolve?

Day 29

You might feel helpless because you don't have all the resources you need; overcomers know that it's important to be resourceful and to use what you have.

While living in a Shaker community and working as a weaver, Tabitha Babbitt watched people struggling to cut wood with a pit saw, which required two users and only cut in one direction. Determined to help, she attached a circular blade to her spinning wheel and invented the much more efficient circular saw.

Babbitt's invention was quickly adopted by her community, and she became known as the "Shaker Shaper." Her invention helped the Shakers to become more efficient in their woodworking and ultimately led to the development of other circular saws that are now used all over the world.

What resources do you have? How can you be more resourceful? What difference can you make with what you have?

Day 30

You might feel like your situation is hopeless; overcomers know that it's important to have hope.

In 1998, The Ericsson phone mobile phone company released a new phone called the T28. The T28 was a huge success, and it helped Ericsson to become one of the leading mobile phone companies in the world.

However, by 2002, Ericsson was in trouble. The company was losing money, and its share price had fallen by 90%. Many people thought that Ericsson was finished.

But the company's CEO, Kurt Hellström, refused to give up. He made some difficult decisions, including laying off a third of the company's employees. He also bet on a new technology called 3G, even though it was unproven and risky.

Hellström's gamble paid off, and Ericsson eventually became profitable again. Today, the company is one of the leading telecom providers in the world.

What is your hope? How will keep yourself encouraged long enough to achieve your hope? What difference can you make with your hope in the lives of others?

Day 31

You may be passionate about your cause but fearful of retaliation; overcomers know that it's important to stand up for what you believe in.

In 2014, at the age of 17, Malala Yousafzai was awarded the Nobel Peace Prize. The Pakistani teen had become notorious for criticizing the Taliban and encouraging young girls like herself to get an education. When she was only 11 years old, she made her first public speech in support of the cause.

However, Malala had to undergo great personal sacrifice to become an advocate for girls' education. In 2012, she was shot in the head by a Taliban gunman while riding the bus home from school. The attack left her in critical condition, but she survived after being airlifted to a hospital in England. She became famous worldwide when she survived an assassination attempt at 15 years old.

Now, Malala is a world-renowned activist and author. She continues to fight for the cause of girls' education. Because of her, many more girls are now attending school in Pakistan and other nations.

What are you willing to risk for your cause? What are you willing to sacrifice?

Day 32

You might feel small in the world; overcomers know that it's important to have a big vision.

Martin Luther King Jr. was one of the most influential visionaries and civil rights leaders in history. He led the civil rights movement and helped to secure the passage of the Civil Rights Act of 1964.

Despite his success, Martin Luther King Jr. faced many challenges his life. He was arrested more than 20 times, and he received numerous death threats.

But King never let the threats stop him. He knew that it was important to stand up for what he believed in, even if it meant risking his own safety. Because of his determination, King is now considered to be one of the most important figures in American history. His senseless death by assassination may have seemed futile, but his living was not in vain.

What is your big vision? What are you willing to do to make it a reality? How will you ensure that your actions outlive you? Is there anything you would be willing to die for?

Day 33

You may feel like people will only remember your last mistake; overcomers know how to overwhelm their mistakes with powerful actions and accomplishments.

Mel Gibson is one of the most successful actors, directors, and producers in Hollywood. He has won two Oscars, and he has directed some of the most popular films of all time.

Despite his success, Gibson has faced many challenges in his life. He was arrested for DUI in 2006, and he made racist and sexist comments that were caught on tape in 2010. These incidents led to him being blacklisted by Hollywood for several years.

Gibson has since apologized for his actions, and he has started to make a comeback in Hollywood. He starred in the hit film Hacksaw Ridge and directed the Oscar-nominated film Apocalypto.

What can you learn from Mel Gibson's story? What are you willing to do to overwhelm your mistakes?

Day 34

You may feel powerless in your situation to bring about a change; overcomers know how to be the change that they want to see in the world.

Christina Aguillera is one of the most successful singers and songwriters of all time. She has won five Grammy Awards, and she has sold more than 50 million albums worldwide.

But Aguilera didn't have an easy childhood. She was raised in poverty, and she experienced abuse from her father and watched him abuse her mother. These experiences led Aguillera to become a passionate advocate for social justice.

In 2001, Aguilera founded the Children's Health Fund, which provides medical care to low-income children. She has also been involved with various other charities, including Amnesty International and the UN World Food Programme.

What is your passion? What are you doing to make a difference in the world? How are you using your platform to help others?

Day 35

You may feel like you are in your darkest hour and that your life won't mean much to others; overcomers know that the good they do today will keep producing for others long after they are gone.

Anne Frank was a Jewish girl who lived in Germany during World War II. When the Nazis came to power, her family was forced to go into hiding to avoid being sent to concentration camps.

For two years, Anne and her family lived in cramped quarters with little food or contact with the outside world. Despite the difficult conditions, Anne kept a diary throughout her time in hiding.

After being discovered by the Nazis, Anne and her family were sent to concentration camps. Anne died of typhus at the age of 15.

Anne's diary was published after her death, and it has since been read by millions of people. Her story is a reminder that even in the darkest of times, there is hope.

What are you going through right now? How can you find hope in your situation? What legacy do you want to leave behind?

Day 36

You could be working really hard right now without receiving very much in return; overcomers know that their time will come and to keep going even when it feels like they aren't getting anywhere.

Estee Lauder is one of the most iconic beauty brands in the world. It is sold in more than 150 countries, and it has a global network of over 3,000 stores.

But Lauder didn't start out as a success. In fact, she was rejected by every cosmetics company she approached when she tried to sell her products.

Lauder persevered, and she eventually found some success when she started selling her products door-to-door. She continued to grow her business, and today Estee Lauder is a multibillion-dollar company.

What are you doing right now that you believe in even though you aren't seeing results? How long are you willing to keep going before you give up? What would it mean for you to achieve your goal?

Day 37

You may have made some mistakes in your past that you are still paying for today; overcomers know that the price they pay for a lesson learned is worth it in the end.

Jamie Oliver is a world-renowned chef, restaurateur, and food campaigner. He has published numerous cookbooks and he has hosted several popular TV shows.

But Oliver didn't always have such a successful career. In fact, he was expelled from school at the age of 16 for disruptive behavior.

Oliver went on to work in several of restaurants, and he eventually started his own restaurant, The Naked Chef. His TV show of the same name made him a household name, and he has since gone on to achieve great success.

What are the pivotal mistakes you have you made that you are still paying for? What have you learned from them? How can you use your experiences to help others?

Day 38

You might be in great danger and fearful about your future; overcomers know to face their fears head on and not give into them.

Novak Djokovac is one of the greatest tennis players of all time. He has won 17 Grand Slam singles titles, and he is currently ranked No. 1 in the world.

Djokovic was born in Serbia, which was going through a civil war at the time. He and his family were constantly in danger, and they had to move around a lot to stay safe.

Despite the dangers that he faced; Djokovic pursued his dream of becoming a professional tennis player. He became the first Serbian player to win a Grand Slam singles title, and he has continued to dominate the sport ever since.

What are you afraid of? What are you willing to do to achieve your dreams? How will you overcome the obstacles in your life?

Day 39

You might feel like you are stuck in a rut and that you will never get out; overcomers know that they can always make a fresh start.

Larry Ellison is the founder and CEO of Oracle, one of the largest software companies in the world. Ellison is a self-made billionaire, and he is currently ranked as the fifth richest person in America.

Ellison dropped out of college after two years, and he struggled to find a job for several years. He eventually found work as a programmer, and he went on to co-found Oracle in 1977.

Despite his success, Ellison has had several setbacks in his life. In the early 1990s, Oracle nearly went bankrupt due to mismanagement. But Ellison was able to turn things around, and Oracle is now one of the most successful companies in the world.

What are you struggling with right now? How can you turn your situation around? What would it take for you to achieve your goals?

Day 40

You may have a dream that feels too big to do it alone; overcomers know that they can achieve anything if they put their mind to it and surround themselves with the right people.

Irv Robbins was the co-founder of Baskin-Robbins, one of the largest ice cream chains in the world.

When he was just starting out, Robbins had a dream to open an ice cream store in every major city in the United States. But he quickly realized that he didn't have the resources to make this dream a reality on his own.

So, he partnered with his childhood friend Burt Baskin, and together they built one of the most successful businesses in history with more than 7000 stores worldwide.

Do you have a big dream? Can a partner or group of partners help you achieve it? Who are they and how and when can you reach out to them?

Day 41

You may feel like you have made too many mistakes to be forgiven; overcomers know that they can start their lives anew.

Georgia Durante is a world-renowned stunt driver who has worked on some of Hollywood's biggest blockbusters.

However, Durante had a troubled childhood and made a lot of bad decisions in her youth. Her exceptional driving skills were discovered in an unusual way that led to her becoming a getaway driver for the mafia. She ended up in prison for drug trafficking, and it seemed like her life was over.

But Durante turned her life around, and she used her skills as a driver to become one of the most sought-after stunt drivers in Hollywood. She has worked on movies like The Fast and the Furious and James Bond, and she is now considered one of the best in her field.

What are the mistakes that you have made? How can you learn from them and make better choices in the future?

Day 42

You might be feeling lost right now and not sure where to go next; overcomers know that it is okay to ask for help and that there is always someone willing to help them find their way.

William Rosenberg was the founder of Dunkin' Donuts, one of the largest coffee and donut chains in the world.

His teenage years were riddled with family issues and due to financial problems, he was forced to leave school to help support his family when he was just in the eighth grade because his family lost their store during the Great Depression. However, by age 21 he had gained a full business education through his work and life experiences. He ultimately became the national sales manager for 100 trucks at an ice cream distribution company. He went on to work for a large steel production company and rose to prominence as the first Jewish trade delegate.

Rosenberg's next move would be one he could not do alone. Feeling confident about starting his own business but knowing he needed help; he borrowed $1000 dollars to add to his $1500 in war bonds and launched his first company. He built his own catering vehicles with sides that rose to reveal sandwiches and snacks stored on stainless steel shelves, an early precursor to mobile catering. Within a few years, he had 200 catering trucks, 25 in-plant locations, and a vending business. When he saw that forty percent of his revenues came from coffee and doughnuts, he started a retail shop focused on those items. The first "Open Kettle" coffee and doughnut shop opened on Memorial Day in 1948; it was renamed "Dunkin' Donuts." Today, Dunkin' Donuts has more than 11,000 stores in 36 countries..

Is there someone who is willing to help you achieve your dreams? What is your plan for reaching out to them to explore the possibilities?

Day 43

You could be facing some tough challenges right now, and you might not know how to overcome them; overcomers know that they can always find a way to overcome the odds.

Theodore Roosevelt was the 26th President of the United States, and he is widely considered to be one of the greatest presidents in history.

Roosevelt was born into a wealthy family, but he struggled with his health throughout his life. He was diagnosed with asthma when he was a child, and he later lost his wife and mother on the same day.

Despite these setbacks, Roosevelt went on to have a very successful career in politics. He was elected as the governor of New York in 1898, and he became the President of the United States in 1901. What are the mistakes that you have made? How can you learn from them and make better choices in the future?

What tough challenges are you still facing now? What is your plan for overcoming them?

Day 44

You may feel like you have failed too many times; overcomers know that they can always learn from their mistakes and that it is never too late to start again.

A failed bank robbery at the age of 20 earned Eugene Brown an 18-year sentence. For some people, that time period may have just as well been a life sentence. However, Brown used his time in prison to garner chess-playing skills and emerged as a chess master.

He started the Big Chair Chess Club, which teaches kids and teenagers to "think before you act." His life has been a lesson of redemption and was turned into a movie entitled *Life of a King* starring Cuba Gooding Jr.

What are you good at? What are you passionate about? How can you turn your talents into a successful business?

Day 45

You may have failed in your past, and you might think that success is in your future; overcomers know that failure is a necessary step to success.

Thomas Edison is one of the most prolific inventors in history, with 1,093 patents to his name. However, at an early age, he was expelled from primary school which meant that he had to learn at home. He was labeled what is today considered a "special needs" child. While Edison was not born into a wealthy family, and he did not have access to the best resources, the very things that society saw as disadvantages, became Edison's advantages.

Thomas Edison went on to become one of the most successful inventors in history. He developed many important technologies, including the light bulb, the phonograph, and the motion picture camera.

Did you know that he failed about 10,000 times before he finally invented the light bulb? In an interview with reporters, Edison once said, "I have not failed. I've just found 10,000 ways that won't work."

What are you working on right now that you haven't been able to achieve yet? What is your plan for persevering until you find a way to succeed?

Day 46

You might have been kicked out, looked over, or stopped short; overcomers know that they will always succeed no matter what.

Michael Jordan is one of the greatest basketball players in history, but he didn't always have such an illustrious career. In fact, he was cut from his high school basketball team.

Jordan went on to play college basketball at the University of North Carolina, where he won a national championship in 1982. He was then drafted by the Chicago Bulls in 1984 and went on to have a highly successful professional career. He won six NBA championships with the Bulls and was named the NBA Finals MVP five times.

What do you need to do to achieve your goals? What steps do you need to take to get there? Are you willing to put in the work required to achieve success?

Day 47

You might feel like no one understands you; overcomers know that sometimes they may have to create the solution, blaze the trail, and start the trend.

Mary Anderson's idea for windshield wipers came to her during a trip to New York City. She was riding in a trolley on a cold, snowy day, and she noticed that the driver had to keep stopping the trolley to wipe the snow off the windshield. Anderson thought there must be a better way, so she designed a device that could clear the windshield while the trolley was moving.

Although she received a patent in 1903, Anderson's windshield wipers failed to become popular before her patent expired. It wasn't until 10 years later that a similar device became standard on cars.

What innovative ideas do you have? How can you turn your ideas into reality? Are you willing to take risks and blaze new trails?

Day 48

Your idea may seem impossible; overcomers know that with God, all things are possible.

When Abraham Lincoln was elected president in 1860, the United States was on the brink of Civil War. The country was deeply divided over the issue of slavery, and Lincoln knew that he had a difficult road ahead.

In his inaugural address, Lincoln appealed to the better angels of our nature and called for unity: "With malice toward none, with charity for all, with firmness in the right as God gives us to see the right, let us strive on to finish the work we are in, to bind up the nation's wounds."

Despite the odds against him, Lincoln persevered and worked tirelessly to heal the divisions in our country. His efforts eventually led to the ending of legalized slavery and the reunification of the United States.

What seems impossible in your life right now? What can you do to turn your situation around? Remember, with God, all things are possible.

Day 49

You might feel like you fell short and missed your opportunity; overcomers know that they can always take one more step.

In 1879, Elisha Gray filed a patent for a device that he called the "telephone." However, another inventor, Alexander Graham Bell, had also been working on a similar device and had filed a patent just hours before Gray.

Many people would have given up at this point, but Gray was determined to continue fighting for his invention. He took his case all the way to the Supreme Court, and in 1885, the court ruled in Gray's favor.

Although he didn't achieve the success he originally hoped for, Gray's tenacity led to some important advances in telecommunications. His work laid the groundwork for modern-day technologies like the radio, television, and cellular phone. Sometimes a mistake may simply be a new invention awaiting discovery.

What are you facing right now that seems impossible to overcome? What can you do to take your work to the next level?

Day 50

You might be at a point where you are not sure if your efforts will matter in the end; overcomers know that it is better to have tried and failed than to have never tried at all.

In 1932, Amelia Earhart became the first woman to fly solo across the Atlantic Ocean. This was a remarkable achievement, but Earhart didn't stop there. She set her sights on an even more challenging goal: flying around the world.

On July 2, 1937, Earhart took off from Miami, Florida, with navigator Fred Noonan by her side. They made it as far as New Guinea before losing radio contact. A massive search effort was launched, but no trace of Earhart or her plane was ever found.

While Earhart's final flight may have ended in tragedy, she inspired other women to pursue their dreams. Her legacy continues to encourage women of all ages to push the boundaries and reach for the stars.

What are you dreaming of doing? What seems impossible right now? How can you take the first step toward making your dream a reality? Remember, it is better to have tried and failed than to have never tried at all.

Day 51

You might feel you have gone as far as you can go on this road because you see roadblocks ahead; overcomers know that there is always a way around, over, or through those obstacles.

Bethany Hamilton was 13 years old when she lost her arm in a shark attack. Many people would have seen this as a tragedy, but Bethany saw it as an opportunity. She returned to surfing one month later. She didn't give up even after falling off her surfboard many times. After two years of dedication, she was rewarded with first place in the Explorer Women's Division of the NSSA National Championships.

Despite the odds against her, Bethany went on to become a professional surfer. She has won multiple championships since and is an inspiration to people all over the world.

Bethany's story is a reminder that there is always a way around, over, or through the obstacles in our lives. No matter what challenges you are facing, don't give up. You can overcome them and come out stronger on the other side.

What are the obstacles in your life right now? How can you find a way around them, over them, or through them?

Day 52

You may have a vision of something that will change the world; overcomers know that it all starts with a single step.

In the early 1900s, the Wright brothers invented the airplane and changed the world forever. But their work didn't stop there. They continued to push the boundaries of aviation, setting new records, and making advances in aircraft design.

In 1903, they became the first people to fly an airplane for more than five minutes. In 1905, they flew for more than an hour. And in 1909, they set a new world record by flying 24 miles in just 38 minutes.

The Wright brothers were not afraid to take risks. They were constantly innovating and expanding the possibilities of what was possible. When you encounter obstacles in your own life, remember them.

What vision are you seeing for which a pattern does not exist? What will be your first steps to making it come to fruition?

Day 53

You may be facing a challenge that requires a life-threatening sacrifice; overcomers know that the risk is worth it if it means saving others.

In 2018, 12 members of the Thai soccer team, known as the Wild Boars, and their coach were trapped in a cave for more than two weeks. Heavy rains had caused the cave to flood, and they were cut off from the outside world.

Rescuers from all over the world came to Thailand to help. But getting the boys out was not an easy task. It took days of planning and preparation before the rescue operation could even begin. And when it did, it was incredibly dangerous.

In the end, all 12 boys and their coach were safely brought out of the cave. It was an amazing feat made possible by the brave rescuers who risked their own lives to save others.

What options do you have to overcome successfully? What resources do you have available to you? How will you use them to overcome your challenge?

Day 54

You may be facing the worst circumstance of your life to this point; overcomers know that this is not the end, but just a new beginning.

Charlize Theron is a successful actress and Academy Award-winning producer. But her life hasn't always been easy. When she was just 15 years old, her father came home drunk and shot and killed her mother in front of her. This tragedy could have derailed Charlize's life. But instead, she used it as motivation to achieve her dreams.

She moved to Hollywood and started auditioning for roles. Eventually, she landed a part in The Cider House Rules, which earned her an Oscar nomination. Since then, Charlize has gone on to star in many popular movies, including Monster, Hancock, The Italian Job, Snow White and the Huntsman, and Mad Max: Fury Road. She is one of the most successful actresses in Hollywood today.

Charlize's story is a reminder that no matter how dark and difficult your circumstances may be, there is always hope for a better tomorrow. You never know what you're capable of until you face your greatest challenge. So don't give up, even when things seem impossible.

What is the darkest and most difficult circumstance you are facing right now? What is your hope for a better tomorrow? What are you willing to do to make that happen?

Day 55

You may feel like calling it quits; overcomers know that quitting is not an option.

In 2006, Navy Seal Marcus Luttrell was on a mission in Afghanistan with his team. They were ambushed by Taliban fighters and outnumbered ten to one. Marcus was the only survivor. He was shot multiple times, had broken bones, and was losing a lot of blood.

The Taliban fighters were closing in on him, and Marcus had to decide. He could stay where he was and fight, or he could try to escape. If he stayed, he would most likely be killed. But if he tried to escape, he would definitely be killed. There was no good option. So, Marcus decided to fight.

Even though the odds were against him, he refused to give up. He fought for hours until finally the Taliban fighters gave up and left him alone. Marcus survived against all odds because he refused to quit.

When you're facing impossible odds, what will you do? Will you give up or will you fight like Marcus did? What is your fight plan?

Day 56

You might feel like you weren't born with what you need; overcomers know that they are exactly who they need to be.

You may not feel capable, but that doesn't mean it's true. You are exactly who you need to be. You have everything it takes to achieve your goals. You must believe in yourself and have faith in your abilities.

Helen Keller was a world-renowned author and speaker, but she wasn't born that way. When she was a baby, she contracted a disease that left her blind and deaf. It would have been easy for Helen to give up. But she didn't.

Helen learned how to communicate using sign language and went on to graduate from college. She wrote multiple books and was even invited to the White House by Presidents Theodore Roosevelt and Woodrow Wilson.

If Helen had given up because she thought she wasn't good enough, she would never have accomplished all the things she did. You are not defined by your circumstances. You can do anything you set your mind to, no matter what anyone else says.

What is that people are saying that you can't do? What do you believe about yourself? What are you going to do to prove them wrong?

Day 57

You may be feeling discouraged; overcomers know that discouragement is only temporary.

Discouragement is a normal part of life. Everyone feels discouraged at times. The important thing is to not let it defeat you. You have to keep moving forward, even when you don't feel like it.

Keanu Reaves is a successful actor who has starred in many popular movies, including The Matrix, Speed, and John Wick. But before he was a Hollywood star, Keanu had experience adversity even as a child. His childhood was full of changes. His dad left when he was three and his mom married four more times after that. He had to change schools often and finally dropped out at 17.

Despite of all the changes and challenges in his life, Keanu never gave up on his dream of being an actor. He moved to Hollywood and auditioned for dozens of roles but experienced many rejections. Keanu could have let the rejection defeat him. But instead, he kept going.

He landed a few roles and eventually his persistence paid off and he landed the role that would change his life forever in the Matrix. If Keanu had given up when things were tough, he would never have become the successful actor he is today.

What are you doing to pursue your dreams? What has been the most difficult part of that journey? What have you learned from it?

Day 58

You may feel like giving up is the easy way out; overcomers know that while it takes more courage to keep going, that courage produces the reward they desire.

It's easy to give up when things get tough. It's much harder to keep going. But overcomers know that the rewards are worth the effort. They also know that giving up is not an option.

Barack Obama was the 44th President of the United States. He was also the first African American to hold that office. But his road to the White House was anything but easy.

Obama faced many challenges and obstacles throughout his life. He grew up without a father and experienced racism firsthand. Despite all of that, he didn't give up on his dreams.

He went on to attend college and then law school. He became a successful lawyer and eventually ran for office. In 2008, he was elected as the 44th President of the United States.

If Obama had given up when things were tough, he would never have become the 44th President of the United States. You may be facing some difficult challenges right now, but don't give up. You have what it takes to overcome them.

What are you facing that seems insurmountable? What obstacles have you already overcome? What can you do to keep going?

Day 59

You might feel like what you desire in life just isn't possible for you; overcomers know that with God, nothing is impossible.

When we face difficult challenges, it's easy to feel like our situation is hopeless. But overcomers know that with God, nothing is impossible.

The Bible tells us in Matthew 19:26, "With God all things are possible." That means that no matter what you're facing, God can help you overcome it. Chris Pratt has come to learn this firsthand. No stranger to faith, he grew up going to church. But it wasn't until he was an adult that he really started to understand the power of God.

Chris struggled with alcohol and drug addiction for many years. He even spent some time living in a van. But he never gave up on his dreams. Chris turned to God and his life has never been the same. He is now one of Hollywood's most successful actors. He credits his success to God. If Chris had given up, he would never have accomplished all that he has. You may feel like your situation is hopeless, but it's not. With God, all things are possible.

What do you need to do to surrender to God? How can you trust that He will help you accomplish it?

Day 60

You're not sure where to start; overcomers know that we must start somewhere.

When we're facing a difficult challenge, it's easy to feel like we're in over our heads. We can look at the situation and feel completely overwhelmed. We don't know where to start or what to do. But overcomers know that we must start somewhere. You may not know what to do, but you can take the first step.

Maya Angelou was a world-renowned author, poet, and civil rights activist. She is someone who knows a thing or two about taking the first step.

In her book, Letter to My Daughter, Angelou talks about how she once had a job as a waitress. She was so afraid of doing it wrong that she didn't want to start. But she realized that she wouldn't accomplish anything if she didn't start somewhere. So she took the first step, and then the next, and eventually she became a successful waitress. We can learn by looking at her life that every time she accomplished anything, she had to begin with a first step.

Maya wrote, "You can't use up creativity. The more you use, the more you have." You may not know where to start, but that's okay. You can't use up creativity. The more you try, the more likely you are to succeed. So, take the first step today, and see where it takes you. You might be surprised at what you can accomplish.

What is the first step you need to take? How will you know if you're successful? What will happen if you don't take the first step?

My Overcomer Story

Let me be vulnerable with you. At the age of 50, I was supposed to retire and cash out on all of my real estate holdings and investments. I had planned to transition into a full-time pastor, build my dream home, and have the dream life. My "dream come true" moment finally came into reach after 30 years. I lost everything in that year; I not only lost my business, the church, and the money machine. I also lost friends, my freedom, and my perspective on life. I shared all of this in my first book, Stripped Naked, and became an Overcomer! Listen, I decided to get up and try again. I was not going down as a quitter, loser, or failure. I cried serious tears, I was shameful, and embarrassed, but the good news is I was forgiven, and I forgave!! I am now an Innovative Publisher, a credible Author, an extraordinary Business Coach, and more importantly, a Kingdom Influencer! If I can do it, **You Can Do It!**

Think it, Say it out loud, and Write it!